STAINED SCRIBBLES

POETRY

SAI SRIRAM

"Hi, Dad!!"

****waves****

for them, my creators for everything they did and still do

To all my relatives who...uhh did nothing but I guess would buy a
copy of this

and to my friends for being there, irritating me, and telling me
that this book is a piece of crap

which I hope is not

****prays to God****

Contents

1. Cursed by Love

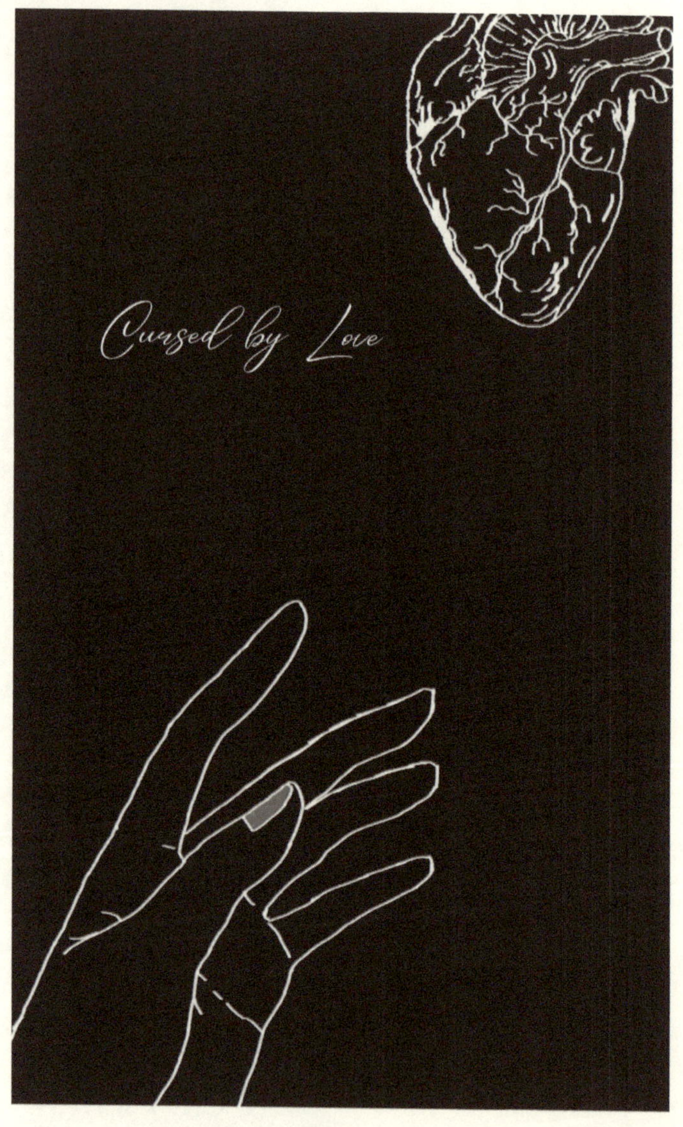
Cursed by Love

Our eyes met for the
first time, mind just
couldn't resist.
That innocent look you
threw,
Day disguised itself into
eternity.

In the crowd of music, let me be your lyric

Under the dim street light, you and me
Hands knitted together
Eyes exchanging promises
Lips speaking not a word, in silence did our walk create music
Beauty she was
By love, we spoke the magic

Calm and tranquil like the moon,
shining from the bosom of her heart
She rained love all over him,
All over the flame of love burning inside him

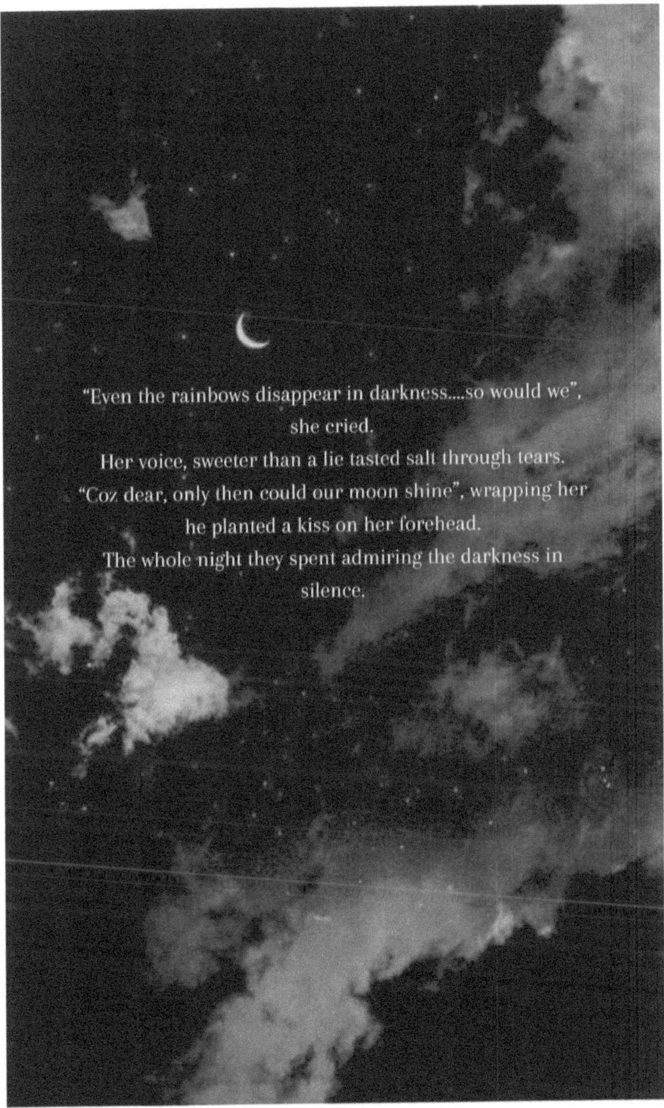
"Even the rainbows disappear in darkness....so would we",
she cried.
Her voice, sweeter than a lie tasted salt through tears.
"Coz dear, only then could our moon shine", wrapping her
he planted a kiss on her forehead.
The whole night they spent admiring the darkness in
silence.

To her imperfections, I fell in love with

Love shrined in darkness,
Raindrops submerged in the sea
Skies of summer seem like its spring
Even the isolated forest clatters with music
does the soil shy away at the glance of each raindrop?
But perhaps,
her shyness is what makes her beautiful and seductive

Unspoken melodies, her voice sang
Searching for lyrics, I died a seven generations
A piece of music you were, lyrists I was
Finding a home in the olive-tanned skin of yours.
Fluttering hair danced with the breeze of rain
All played instruments of love on their own
In the tune,
Of your unspoken melody.

It was under that crying moon,
I witnessed a dandelion
blooming on the top of a rock
Tears of the moon sprinkled on its petals,
With a blush, she danced
The rock silently enjoyed, admiring her,
dancing on his spine.
Great warriors had it witnessed,
Harsh climates had it undergone
but that was the first time he fell in love
With himself.

"What is love?" asked the boy
"Love is the sun giving its light to the moon though knowing
it cannot be reciprocated,
Love is the waves coming to kiss the shore though being
pushed away every time,
Love is time, giving moments to live with,
Love is change, for being the only constant,
Love is karma, for gifting us what we deserve
Love is death, for giving us an eternal rest
Love is you, Love is me, Love is god and
Love is life", replied the old man.

SAI SRIRAM

Sow my seed in your soul,
Hug me to lose control,
Checkmate me lavishly, let the pain dim, and depart
From the atrium of the heart

Day and night, teary-eyed
Wilted eyes, sleep deprived
From head to heal, this love bug
doesn't heal
The ecstasy, love rains
Only as a fool, could one gain

Hearing the voice of your melody, so seductive and
whimsy
My heart feels a mystic bliss,
so much too fancy

When our eyes do the talking, what could she say?
Words fail her,
piercing her with his gaze
The heart does a waltz

Unspoken desires, mornings that never dawn,
Nights that never end
And our drops of sweat that never dry,
Un-partitioned moments under the blanket sky

Her lips, that part to bloom and beckon
Have endless letters inscribed.
And even before he could respond, she
evaporates like a dream,
Melting into him

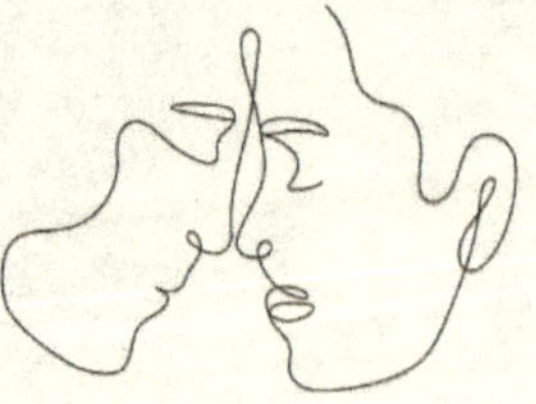

You, my dear, the showering moon,
won't the sky slip and dance?
Burning desires need to be felt and touched

Caressing your face like a flower bud,
to inhale your scent
Even before I could get drunk with your pollen
You bloomed into a flower,
And the scorching heat withered away

Under the full moon
night,
As rain drips down from
your form
I imagined us

In this world of chaos, her beauty he witnessed. Great men
under penance, lost themselves seeing her beauty. Nature
tried competing with her. Failing each time, it cried rain,
and yet her smile, they admired. Her heart was made from
oozing honey, and her body painted from the brush of
lightning amazed him. Enthralled under the morning sun,
he stood awestruck

You are a fool when you are in love

Stephen Chbosky once said
some moments make us feel infinite.
You and me, our first meet
A "Hi" jumped from my mouth.
Hearing it, your cheeks blushed.
Ears twinkled, eyes expanded.
And a second later, your lips carved a smile
Hi", your voice fondled my ears
Eyes excited, but seeing yours, it fell in love.
Not once, not twice, but an infinite times
"Our story has begun"
We screamed in silence. A moment of a minute, a
memory of a lifetime

• 25 •

Shattered stars glued together
Painted with a pinch of the dark sky
Sculpted inside the seduction of the bright moon
Your eyes are, Darling

And then, at last wrapping hands around me,
You placed your lips on mine
Forgetting the world around us,
A good one minute we lived

Kiss me till I'm dizzy, my love
Let the quest for love end in the silence
of sounds

Your form is a sculpture itself.
Pearls and gems sunk in envy.
Seeing you they mumble,
"Gods were too stingy"
Even the angles stumble.
Made from the brush of lightning,
rainbows cry in joy for a queen, found at last.
Oh dear, this isn't fair,
All this beauty, none could handle
And yet,
I knelt with a ring in my hand,
A blush on your face.
Words were not needed for the eyes did all the talking
A beautiful journey of selfless love has begun.

With the moon booming, your serpentine hips gleaming
Blushing cheeks like a slice of ginger,
Dash a pink shyness to linger.
Seeing you my lips tingle
Flower-scented, senses heightened, till my lips throb
I am a work of art painted sublime to disturb your sleep all
the time

2. Whittled by Melancholy

Whittled by Melancholy

The mind started acting, perhaps like a wet mirror
Seeing those magical eyes of yours,
Heart sank to deep depths
Spinal spiraled down
Her look mesmerized him
Her name, still unknown
And "US", a term not yet created
Oh cupid, hit them both the next time

Making us meet, the cupid sowed a seed of love.
Growing into a root, he went deep inside
Knowing not that you were the bud, the world's awaiting to
witness.
Love blinded us, and for you to bloom and shine
I'd go to the depths of darkness

A Thousand times and more

Whispering your name a thousand times,
I stood alone in the graveyard of love
Witnessing your golden brown eyes fade away,
Mine blinded itself.
Feeling your fragrance, no longer, now deceased
Mine stopped breathing.
Seductive lips, yours no longer
Curvy face, wrinkled and dried,
Mine poured rains of tears.
Soul wanted to shout, no wonder kept quiet,
For your slumber not to be disturbed.
Death ain't going to sunder us
Coz I love you
A thousand times and more

Every wave flutters, narrating a story of the hidden sea they
carry.
The six seasons pass with the melancholy of pain,
The world experiences.
Crying rain fills itself with grief, and sinks
Inside the painting of blue, the life

Lost in the space of endless blue thoughts,
I looked in the mirror,
My skin bloomed flowers,
Eyes cried poetry.
Curly hair swirled into each other in sadness,
Hands disintegrated to ashes,
Burnt and burned,
Heart pierced through layers of thoughts
I watched as my life collapsed

Fainted inside sorrow, my heart sunk to its bottom
Limbs crumbled and shrunk, breathing pain
Standing alone from the crowd of life,
will my soul be considered?
Perhaps not,
Eyeballs floated in salt,
more than an ocean could ever carry
And the soul held its saltiness
Is this a dream?
Or a cursed reality?
Let it get eroded if this is a dream
from the cursed reality of life

At eighty and plus, half body paralyzed
Wrinkled skin, reflecting paleness
Eyes losing sight
Broken spectacles
I held and with a pen,
I scribbled, one last letter to your grave
"In soon time, we'll meet again to knit hands for eternity"

Once again life hit me with grief,
But this time I didn't bleed blood
I bled poetry

Running in my blood,
Veins filled with words, blood sunk in feelings, and heart
flew up
Mind went high, drugged with poetry
I closed my eyes
Colorless memories brought colorful poetries

• 41 •

This morning I dreamt of you
Walking through the shores of a colorless sea.
Holding hands with someone else
Your beauty, I saw another soul admiring
A pinch of possessiveness brushed my heart

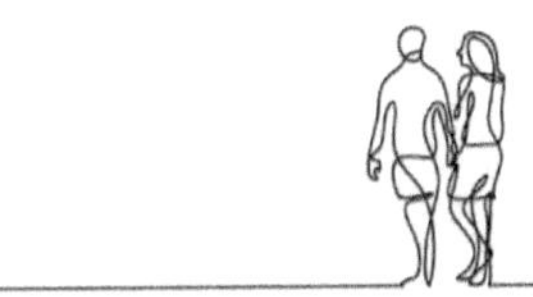

An unknown pain, a hopeless confusion
Looped inside time, pulled him in
The fear of losing her washed his face
Even before he could know her

Neither does love fade away like a forgotten story
Nor does it get forgotten like an unworthy puzzle mystery

Oh these strings search fingertips longing for
unknown tunes

He asked her to spare her sleep for him
She refused,
Now he entered her sleep with the false key called dreams
While searching for the right words
He taught her the language of silence but
Was ignorance a part of it too?

The moments that melt away cursing your absence
Seem like years
The heart has blended into yours
Witness my breath whisper your name
A thousand times

Step by step he's changing
Yet this life doesn't change
Falling short for words, slipping here and there
The mind never gets stable
Hidden in the baffling memories
Flying up and down like a kite
Getting caught in the arms of the future
Even time has forgotten him
Every moment and every ignorance
The secret is in the heart,
Hidden deep inside
Melting away with the flak of time
Why is this wordsmith's path so different?
Like a pen writing and stopping
I'm too hidden in the breath of future

The never-ending poem of silence
Is high on this smoggy eve
Only in this solitude could I breathe
Veins in my body
Like the ropes of a swing sway to the lullaby
The silence sings

• 49 •

When you were offering those teardrops to me so hot in
their gems of stone
Was it my anticipation for love?
Long dead and crumbled to earth,
They began to adorn themselves with new leaves

Multitudes of melancholy inside me
Like someone breaking the surface
Of water and grasping breath after almost drowning
I burst out of the confines of language
Creating a new one for the bittersweet
And without the barrier of words
Did I finally understand
"I'M GONNA MISS YOU"

One bright, we set like
The sun in November
It was late in the day
When dusk fell
And the Book of Us came to an end
Readers closed the page
And rucked us onto a shelf
Old and forgotten
A story told and read

Legs walking through tears,
melodies of love went a long way

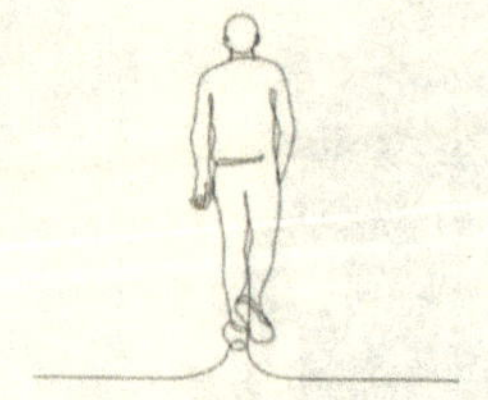

Eyes are looking for you
But tears in between act as a painful hurdle

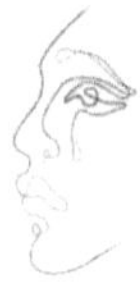

Are love just dreams?

• 55 •

Draped in clouds, you drift away
when I seek you

Daydreaming all night,
I forgot to sleep
I felt numb while you are away
Longing for you, my tears cry
This small pain in my heart gets mesmerized,
When your eyes embrace
We met in dreams
Not once, but a many time
Oh girl, I wish you were real

Our lips pampered primal unhampered
Even time lost its consciousness
A beautiful moment
I sowed in my heart
The one that couldn't be grown

Colorless rainbows blossomed when memories washed
over me

Architecture of Absence

Life has mastered
The architecture of absence
Leaving us alone at the end of the day
Is all has it done
Perhaps, the architecture of absence
A beautiful term it is,
You open the door of your home
A room filled with nothing but an absence
Absence of people, absence of love
Absence of care and
Absence of YOU

It's a state of mind
Where you're neither happy nor sad
But empty and upset
You miss people badly
And yet wanted to be disappeared from them

I sat down staring at the blue sky from my
ajar window,
Little dreams brushed off expectations
With the colors borrowed from the rainbows.
Little did I know was the rain that marched
towards me
Dressing blue all over
Life crippled down into the ocean of tears
Salty, they were
Melancholy all over and in a second,
I was back
Staring at the same blue sky
Filled not with dreams but with melancholy

To the skies,
Touch me, drench me all over the rain
Let this pain and suffering drain off
And I could fall in love with you once again

Jumping out of the eyes,
Rolling down the skin, flying in the air
Carrying tons of emotions
Salty in its nature, escaping the reality of grief
Took birth, terrible tiny tears.

3. Blessed with Insomnia

Blessed with Insomnia
Shattered by Memories

• 67 •

Teary eyes spilled salty all over
Sun-dried lips scattered words sober
Being the devil, I lost my angel
Into hell from the heaven

• 68 •

Life broke my soul into half
Bleeding pain, it smiled
"ATLAST.... I die PEACEFULLY"

In love with hope, two years passed since your eyes, I
admired. Waiting for you in the loop of time, twenty years
passed, since your lips bit mine. The glass of wine, we held
while our lips fused. Now everything's gone, soul and heart,
torn. Two hundred years passed, yet my broken soul
searches for you,
I pain with hope, I stood crying in front of your grave. You
held my hand, alas. To heaven, we walked together. We're
indeed made for each other darling. In this world not, but in
heaven.

Too poisonous it is, love. But the joy in the
pain of suffering,
The poor soul once drugged, all it does is
Hopelessly wait

Hands dissolve in wounds, depressed in loneliness

At the end of the day, memories don't help us
They hurt the most

I was the star abandoned by the lords in heaven,
Floating as a lonely cloud, in the fall of dusk
I wandered through the pain
Oh girl, I turn into a dew of divinity in you whom pearls of
beauty shred.
For I'm blessed
Lotuses weakened by our chitchats
and the moon in its ethos
The tunes of spring they play along with the sweet magical
cuckoo's murmurs make up this musical moon-lit night
I longed for.
Chords of love turned to melody
like the enchantment of dew.
You'll see me one day on this lonely road of our
memories.
Someday, you'll search for my footprints and still
My soul would whisper to you
"I have loved you"

Breathing becomes hard when you cry,
Trying to swallow the memories,
Heart and lungs suffer pain,
Legs tremble,
Mind in a blank state, silence it desires
Yet the screaming heart yearns for you.
Eyes longing to cry, but no tears could it shed
Holding your photo, admiring your smile
Cursing your absence, remembering your voice
The way you breathe, the way your eyes blink
All this makes the heart much worse
What sort of madness is this oh girl?
I never knew, missing you would be killing me alive

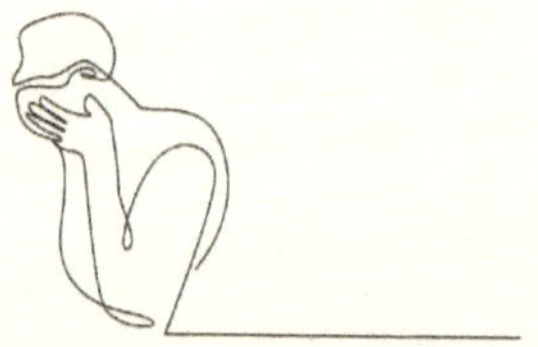

The scholar of life defined death
as the pleasure of destiny

Only when we cry and burn in the
saltiness of pain
Do our rainbows bloom

With each sunrise and sunset,
With each petal of the dandelion fading away,
Time flies.
Yet my long-lost love stays still,
Filled with pain, waiting for you with a hopeless hope
It strangles me into suffering
And I'm no longer able to survive
This little love, my soul nurtured
Has now grown into a huge tree.
Bearing leaves of grief, no fruit could be found.
Watering it every day with tears,
I ended up ruining myself

The thirst for life dead in my thoughts
Hearts like a coward
Ain't interested in sharing
A fool under the celestial lights
Searching for hope, though, knowing its dead
Legs walked through tears,
Pain grows in the tip of my fingers
Melodies of life lost in the stream of sadness
Thoughts of tomorrow burn inside n' out

Her beauty still mesmerizes him. Her preciousness caresses
his heart. Understanding her thoughts, an earthquake he
feels inside. His lyric on her wood, their skin fused amid the
Garden of Eden, They made love.
Now a stranded forest, he has become.
Deforested and separated, until a kid one day
Scribbled their name, "Adam and Eve were here"
Their sons too, composed lyrics on woods
Her beauty they still admire and his sin, they still repeat.
Love has become a disease.

Tears started showering,
This time love couldn't resist
Soul bled pain, ribcage rippled apart
Limbs fell down, disintegrated
Heart dwindled and stonkered
With closed eyes, they stood
As death approached.

Letter to Her

Little did you know, that I loved you.
That someone was there for you.
But you wouldn't have, coz you were busy running
while I built you a castle of dreams
It's all become painful now.
They have become strands and
swirl around my neck,
Strangle me to death or they turn into a glass jar
and pull me inside,
Suffocating me to death,
and throwing my corpse into space
But unknowingly, I left my heart with you
And no matter, how our worlds end
I don't wanna snatch it from you
Coz it's you and with you, I'm madly in love

Dear dreams have a break. Mind's exhausted already
Expectations never happen,
and disappointments all over
The soul too, always sober. Heart yet couldn't
understand
Blurred by dreams, slapped by reality
Repeating on a loop of time

.

Tired, lost, and failed, feels like I need a sleep.
A sleep, from which I need not have to wake up.
Reality is too overrated.
I just wanna sleep and dream maybe

In a crowded park, I sat on a broken bench.
Drizzling rain and umbrellas all wide open
I drenched, and so did the bench
For we lost you
No more "us"
Our bench, no more alive. Covered with leaves,
bleeding tears
Memories we sculpted on it, are all gone.
The bench, you, and I
Missing us, missing you
We cried, remembering Chaplin's words,
"None sees your tears in the rain"

Evil God / Vicious Devil

Oh, devil, I have come here mooching
For this nugatory life which is constantly in search of
materialistic desire
Is now haunting me.
Every moment I'm living, the woe, the agony
Not once, not twice
God made me take innumerable deaths
Now that I'm here
Where shall I go beg?
He, the creator of this world is making me the puppet
For this illogical drama called life.
Here I'm trying to know the truth, bargaining for death
This mortal body is now changing
From growing god,
to anxiously wait to decimate
and bathe in the numen's blood

4. The Healing

The Healing

They say everything happens for a reason,
Maybe they were right
*****Hope comes inn*****

Mystical memories painted bliss all over me,
The hanging hope in the cold breeze of life felt
warm for the first time.
Celestial moon danced with drizzling rain, gleaming
through the playing stars of comets.
Soul went into a state of trance.
Things around me stood still while I floated up
against gravity.
Sorry, Newton, there are things
physics couldn't marry
Two more minutes left for me to be pushed back
into the life of reality but good lords,
The loop mode was active.
My heart skipped a beat when the lyrics pierced
inside my skin, giving chills all over my body.
Instruments screamed in its melodies making the
mind high.
The world around me faded as I vanished from it,
entering a third dimension
In my headspace,
I live everyday hearing music

Coz, after all, the pain our soul carried,
Untold stories our spine cried,
We got to move on and this time
Life seemed to be beautiful,
Giving us time to breathe,
It lets us relax
It lets us live

And at last,
Just like the end of an ice cream, life is....

Well, you have made it to the end.
Though it's a very short journey of holding my heart in your
palms.
I just wanna thank you, guys, for givin' in your effort to reach
this part,
the one where the book knows it's going to be rucked inside
the shelf again but
with the satisfaction that it's loved and read.
just close your eyes, take a deep breath, and puff out all the
thoughts messing with your poor soul.
the truth is that whatever happens, whatever steps you take to
free yourself
from overthinking, from all the pain, the grief, people have
caused
you end up hurting yourself again, and again and again.
there is no cure for this blessing but there is a drug
Irony calls it poetry.
Take a moment, look around, and realize that everything that
surrounds you has a poem hidden inside waiting for someone who
could dig it out and own it.
Be that someone.
Cause one day, everything would change. life would be better
and you would realize that you were a poetry yourself!
Thanks for reading.

About The Author

Sai Sriram grew up under the aesthetic celestials of this modern world hearing music and scribbling literature. Film-making and films fed him interest and enough curiosity for his pen to bleed ink on paper. Just to shake things up, he does an undergraduate program in biosciences and eats ice creams for no reason.

www.ingramcontent.com/pod-product-compliance
Lightning Source LLC
Chambersburg PA
CBHW062234150726
47991CB00006B/2575